The Receptionist Handbook

By
Lisa Harmon

This Book is Dedicated to My
Mother

who taught me
everything I know
about working in an
office.

ACKNOWLEDGEMENTS

This book could not have been written without the help of Thomas Hannigan and Lance Rossing. Their generosity of time, patience and support can not be rivaled.

Table of Contents

INTRODUCTION

ROTUS, (Receptionist Of The United States) Darienne Page, joined the Obama campaign upon returning from her military service. Previously, she had worked as a paralegal in Baghdad, taking depositions in the Abu Ghraib prison. She was close to her commander then, as is evident by the bracelet she wears which has his name inscribed.

Sadly, he was killed when enemy fire struck his helicopter in late 2003. She was recently quoted in The New York Times as saying "He taught us to lead, but to lead with a smile and be calm under pressure," she said. "A lot of lessons that I learned in the Army help me here. There is a lot that goes on that I have to do with a smile even if I really don't want to."

There isn't a receptionist out there who hasn't felt that way at one time or another. Too often this position is viewed as unimportant, which is simply untrue. And while most of us will never have daily interaction with the President of the United States, like receptionist Darienne Page, we are, nevertheless, important to the success of the organizations we serve.

What makes a great receptionist? The same thing that makes an English butler. It's shining brightly with dignity and grace, in keeping with the receptionist role. It's anticipating people's needs before they express them. It's taking initiative, yet knowing the parameters in which to do so. It's mastering the English language, so as to speak clearly and effectively. It's displaying proper etiquette, and decorum. It's pride in appearance, and pride in the company. It's showing kindness and respect to both the CEO and janitor, equally. It's more than meets the eye. It's about shaping the voice, the face, and the branding of an institution. In short, it's hard work!

Regardless of the type of office environment in which we work, our look, our speech, and the way we move about, are all being observed and evaluated by everyone.

First impressions rarely fade. To enjoy success, lets take a look at what makes a great receptionist.

CHAPTER 1
FINDING THE RIGHT JOB

To provide a clearer illustration of the receptionist role, I have identified three types of receptionists and three types of reception desks.

3 types of receptionists:

1.) The veteran
2.) The ambitious passer-by
3.) The first time worker

Phrases employers will look for during the interview:

- "I see myself as a career receptionist"
- "I'm very interested in the insurance business"
- "I really hope you consider me for this position"

If you've just used the first phrase, you've indicated to the prospective employer that you're a veteran. You enjoy what you do and are looking to stick with it for several years if not your lifetime. If you bring the skills needed, and the employer is looking for longevity in his receptionist, this can be the perfect match.

If you've used the second phrase, you've indicated to the

prospective employer that you are an ambitious passer-by, and you have an interest beyond reception work. It's fine if you're looking to use the front desk as a foot in the door to start your non-reception career. However, be prepared for the response, as they may ask for a concrete time commitment.

"Yes, we love to promote from within, however keep in mind we require a minimum of one year of service before allowing movement into other available positions".

A statement such as this can not be ignored. It's best to be honest about what you really want, even if it results in a mutual decision by both you and the employer to move on to another candidate. But if you are willing to reconsider your career time line and are willing to stick it out for a full year to get that next opportunity, then making this commitment should be fine.

If you've jumped the gun in your first interview and blurted out the third phrase, all is not lost. While you did just indicate to the employer your lack of experience, with an over abundance of enthusiasm towards an entry level position, the employer could surprise you. They may decide to invest time in shaping your skills, rather than immediately rejecting your inexperience. If this happens, you're in! But don't give up if this scenario doesn't play out.

There is a job out there for everyone. You have to start somewhere. You may even frame your inexperience as an asset, by explaining that your eagerness to learn will result in an an easier training period. The employer may recognize that by starting with a clean slate, there will be fewer bad habits to break, and even fewer times when a battle of wills may ensue... *Well, that's not how we did it at ABC Contractors.*

An inexperienced employee can be exactly what an employer wants, and a first time job may come quicker than you think!

There are 3 types of reception desks:

- single service
- dual service
- combination service

The single service desk is a one man operation. Answering the phone and greeting visitors is it's primary function. Generally these desks are referred to as *switchboards* and the receptionist as an *operator.*

The dual service desk is a shared desk, employing two receptionists. High call volume and more complex calls creates a work load which necessitates two people.

Working a desk such as this requires a unique combination of personalities willing and able to be flexible.

The good side is, it is a self sustaining pod. Breaks and lunches are alternated which gives more freedom and flexibility to the front desk staff. It also removes the burden off of other office workers who fill in when the receptionist is away.

The down side is sharing the spotlight, the praise, and the work. It can be challenging at times if one receptionist is a neat freak and the other is a mess. It is also harder to pinpoint errors when one cannot distinguish between the two receptionists.

The combination service desk is typically one person taking care of a multitude of tasks with a light to moderate call volume. This is the most satisfying, as it gives the receptionist more challenges, and a sense of accomplishment.

Whether you're just starting out, or you're a veteran, each person brings to the front desk a unique set of skills, needs and desires for the future. Identifying these can help you avoid the wrong employer and instead, discover the perfect job for you.

CHAPTER 2
HYGIENE, CLOTHING AND IMAGE

Personal **Hygiene** is a delicate subject, yet an essential part of working in a service or support role. Receptionists are greeting the public on behalf of the organization with whom they are employed, and cleanliness is crucial.

People aren't perfect though, and sometimes it's stressful to be at a reception desk if you aren't feeling well, or you are going through personal turmoil.

However, the important thing to remember, is to see your image as part of the job. Image is a big part of being a receptionist. Although it's frequently overlooked, it should be given careful consideration.

You are part of the lobby. And as a receptionist you should be the star of that lobby, shining brighter, and appearing cleaner than anything else in that space.

You are the face of the company, and that "face" should be clean. You need not spend money on elaborate treatments. A simple at home method is more than sufficient to keep your skin glowing.

To get you started, here are two simple regimens you might want to try:

- Wash your face with soap and warm water.
- Apply witch hazel all around your face and neck using a cotton ball. Pure witch hazel is a natural substance and the largest ingredient of the expensive "toners" sold at department stores. You can find it for about $2.50 at the drugstore and it accomplishes the same thing as the expensive products.
- Splash with ice water.
- Apply moisture as needed.

- Apply cold cream. (any brand sells for about $3.00 at the drugstore)
- Place a steaming wet cloth over your face and let it set until cool.
- Rinse the cloth in hot water and wipe the remainder of cold cream from your face.

As a receptionist, your budget is of constant concern, so unless it is summer time, skip the pedicure and go straight for the manicure. Rarely do people see you from your waist down, and in the winter months you have boots and closed toed shoes to shield your feet from view. Your hands, however, are the most visible part of your body, second only to your hair and face, and should be kept clean.

Keep in mind, a manicure is not just for women anymore, and men need to be just as meticulous about fingernails and hand appearance.

Shop and compare. Most of the time the prices in the suburbs are far less than downtown. If you have a bus pass, taking time out of your Saturday to travel outside the city for a less expensive manicure, is worth it.

Hair is a sore subject for me as I am a cancer survivor and was bald for a good portion of one year while still working as a receptionist.

So, I invested in a beautiful wig that matched my former long brown hair. And believe it or not, many people in my company did not even notice the change. They assumed I had straightened or conditioned my hair, and many were not even aware I had cancer.

Although it was my most trying time to date, I took pride in the fact that I had mastered my receptionist "image" to such a level that I could hide even the most serious of appearance issues.

Some cancer survivors disagree with this approach and proudly display their bald heads. That's OK too. However, comfort is most important, and hiding under a wig worked best for me. Each person should make their own decision. Do what works for you. Don't worry about what others are doing. In this instance, there is no "right way."

If you aren't bald, remember that basic cuts are the cheapest to maintain, and long hair is even less of a chore. If your hair is long enough you can trim it yourself, and save hundreds in beauty salon visits. Rather than the salon, invest in quality products.

If trimming your own hair is too scary, consider choosing your local barber shop instead of opting for the mega salon at the shopping mall. A barber is a lot cheaper and faster. Both men and women are beginning to frequent the barber, and it's a great way to save money.

Ultimately, it really doesn't matter whether you are a man or a woman, or you choose the expensive route to beauty or the corner drug store. The bottom line is, you should be neat, clean and free of dandruff, dirty fingernails, and skin blemishes.

Clothing is a personal choice, yet the choices should be made within the confines of your employer's official dress code. If you are unsure about what that may be, it is always a good idea to ask your human resources representative. Most of the time, an employer will have an employee handbook, from which you can find the necessary information.

There are three types of basic "dress codes" in corporate America today:

- business dress
- business casual
- casual

<u>Business dress</u> refers to suits and ties for men, and pant suits, skirt suits, or dresses for women. Pants worn in the business dress environment should always be worn as part of a suit. This rule applies to both genders.

<u>Business casual</u> can be difficult to judge. The basic rule of thumb is follow the leader. The executive support person generally sets the tone for the office and to follow his or her lead is the best defense against a fashion mistake.

<u>Casual</u> in a business setting sounds like "anything goes", but it isn't. Generally, for men it means khaki pants and tropical or plaid button down shirts. The

same is true for women. Sweaters or sweater vests are also nice for either gender. Mini shorts, tube tops, or cut off jeans are appropriate in only two locations on earth: the beach and your own back yard. (And even then it's questionable). Some longer shorts are smart and stylish. These would be acceptable if worn with a blouse, top or sweater and accented with non-athletic shoes and dress socks.

In the past I've heard the phrase "window dressing" used in a derogatory way. But in the case of reception work it is not. It is the very core of what we do as receptionists. We are the face, the voice, the representative of the company we serve, and it is our highest priority to maintain a stellar appearance.

The irony is, the least paid person in the company is expected to look like the highest paid person, but it can be achieved if you do your homework on clothes.

Other clothing tips

Women: Never show cleavage. It doesn't move you up the ladder, it pushes you out the door. Just say no to cleavage. If your favorite dress is borderline appropriate, try using tailor tape, which is found at most fabric stores, or just a couple of safety pins.

Men: Tight clothing is a big no-no. Even if you have to have your clothes hand tailored in a small Panamanian village, do not skimp on this requirement. Loose clothing also aids in staying fresh and clean and cool.

Hosiery: The requirements have changed over the years. As a person who has worked in corporate America for a number of years now, I can state with confidence that hosiery is not required in a business casual office. Because most offices today have adapted the business casual look, this would be correct most of the time.

A clean and neat appearance: It's always a winning look regardless of your fashion tastes. And when in doubt, remember to look around you and adapt your image to match other successful employees at the company, but within the framework of your own personal style.

Final thoughts on clothes...

Do use your sewing skills to make dresses, skirts and blouses.

Do scour the second hand shops for bargains. (A $2.00 blouse taken to the dry cleaners for $10.00 is still a lot less than $38.50 retail.)

Do choose colors wisely. Black, gray and brown are all colors that go with everything and will stretch your fashion dollar.

Do choose fabrics wisely. Stay away from thick heavy wool or very thin chiffon. Instead, go for a woolen feel polyester or rayon that is not too thin and not too heavy, so it will work in all seasons.

Do shop online. There are many deals to be had for the savvy shopper, and this is usually a faster and sometimes less impulsive way to shop for clothing.

Don't buy a trendy summer dress that can only be worn a few weeks before going out of style.
Don't buy full retail price!
Don't buy cheap just because it's cheap. Sometimes investing in two good pieces and building your wardrobe around it with discount blouses, and scarves works well.
Don't skimp on shoes. If you think no one will notice your stinky broken down shoes, think again. Inevitably you will be wearing these relics on the exact day the IT guy needs to crawl around under your desk to fix your computer. Don't risk that embarrassment. Just buy a new pair. They don't have to be $300.00 Italian beauties. A simple $20.00 pair will do. If a new pair is not possible, remember that scuffs and worn heels are easily repaired at a cobbler for little cost.

What is **image**? It's a ballet of
personality, looks, and everyday
movement that meld into one
physical you! Poise, elegance,
and charm are all important
aspects of image.

The easiest way to learn about
image is to study those people
whom have mastered a great image
and projected the epitome of
correctness.

The first and foremost example is
Grace Kelly. If you watch the
classic movie "Rear Window" you
will not only see a woman who is
impeccably dressed, you will see
elegance and charm as it should
be: fluid, flawless, fascinating.
Watch her enter and leave a room.
Watch her sit in a chair. Watch
her hands as she strolls or stands
to speak. Listen to her voice and
the language she uses. You can
learn a great deal by studying
Grace Kelly.

Another person with flawless taste is of course, the late Princess Diana. Although pegged as a painfully shy woman, she exuded charm and grace far beyond her years. Even though she was a Princess and knew which outfit to wear to each occasion and how to greet and bid farewell, she did not come by this naturally. She was schooled in these skills. Fine manners are not born from royal blood, they are learned.

Many components make up our image, and the more pleasing we are, the more likely we will become the successful receptionist we hope to be.

"May I help you?"
"May I take a message?"
"May I offer you coffee?"
"May I take your coat?"
. . . Mother may I

Before we look at what skills make up reception work, lets discuss the receptionist role at it's most basic level: To receive.

A receptionist is the liaison between client and company, between vendor and company, between the general public and company. It is a portal where most inquiries initiate. From there, reception work becomes a series of relay systems, using phone and email to relay what is said, given or requested to the appropriate colleague.

The reception desk could also be categorized as a transfer station, transferring paper, voice and person from the entry point to the destination.

What makes this job so challenging is that most paper, voices and persons don't always know their destination, causing the receptionist to balance accommodation with research, diplomacy and speed.

These are the core reception skills needed to excel at the front desk:

1. Answering the phone in a friendly manner
2. Taking messages effectively
3. Greeting guests promptly and respectfully
4. Resolving conflict
5. Mastering the art of staying calm under pressure

Answering the phone in a friendly manner can be tedious and it is easy to slip into a rote method with little feeling. The receptionist who can fight this, and always maintain a helpful, friendly tone will be the most successful.

The basic rule for answering multiple calls is to answer

quickly and to place each call on hold. Then go back to the callers one by one to assist them in the order the calls were received. Answer the ringing, then answer the questions.

Sometimes an internal caller will phone in between outside callers. In this case, handle the external callers first. If it's a quick question, and you have the number right in front of you, go ahead and disrupt the order, to reduce the number of callers holding.

Sometimes internal callers will get cranky with you, but remaining calm and adhering to your order of service will eventually gain you respect and understanding from your fellow colleagues.

Some internal callers are simply being lazy and don't want to take the time to look up the number themselves. This is fine, since your job is to provide reception service to everyone. However, if they abuse the system, it may be time to speak up and explain that at times it can be very busy at the front desk and that you'd be happy to provide them with a new directory if they have misplaced theirs. Usually the colleague will be grateful for your extra effort, and at the same time it helps you too, by eliminating unnecessary calls.

Taking messages effectively means writing legibly, repeating the information back to the caller to ensure accuracy, and finally relaying the message timely to the recipient. Email or instant message is a great way to get the message out quickly, and have it time stamped and documented so there is little confusion if follow up is required. Leaving a voice mail is also useful, however, putting something in writing is your best defense against future problems.

The three most important items on a message are WHO called, WHEN did they call, and WHAT is their phone number. Never rely on "Oh he knows my number." Always ask for the number no matter what the response. Often times if you mention that a return call may happen quicker if the caller provides his number, then he will be happy to give it again. It's also a good idea to include your name or initials as the message taker, and other pertinent information the caller may have given.

Greeting guests promptly and respectfully requires constant monitoring of the doors and entry ways. A proper greeting begins at the door, not at the desk. Keep your head up and your eyes and ears open, always remaining aware of what is going on around you. Be cognoscente of your own voice level also, as there may be stairwells and corners where others are standing or listening. Never gossip at the front desk, as inevitably the very person you are disparaging is listening down the hall.

Being aware of your surroundings means staying alert. This is best achieved by walking outside the building on your breaks and lunches and readjusting your eyes, your mood and getting fresh air and a snack.

Being respectful requires practice. You must learn to watch and listen for cues from a person's body language and voice to help with your responses. If someone is in a hurry or reading the paper, keep your conversation to a minimum so as not to disturb him. If someone is chatty, keep the conversation going on light subjects such as their travel to the office, the weather, etc. Refrain from political, religious or other hot subjects unless directly asked your opinion.

Respect is also shown by always maintaining fair treatment. If you treat the executive differently than the secretary and still different from the building maintenance man you risk losing integrity and respect from others. Always smile at everyone even when you may not feel like doing so. If they don't smile back, let them go, and don't take it personally. A warm, friendly greeting makes such a difference. Think about when you walk into your doctors office or your grocery store, and think about how the service is and how you are treated. When you are ignored or spoken to abruptly it is not pleasant. So when imagining this, understand that during your work day the role is reversed and the person on the receiving end of your curt tone may not like it either. They may even speak up to your supervisor. It's easier to be pleasant to everyone than deal with the consequences of poor performance.

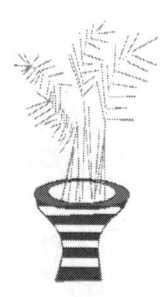

Resolving conflict is tough. There is no easy road to conflict resolution. But there are good practices. It's like yoga. It's a process. And to master this, one must embrace conflict as a time to learn and grow, rather than an unpleasant experience to be avoided or contained. Conflict provides opportunity, and here are a few ways to handle conflict:

- Find common ground, and arrive at a consensus on the result desired.
- Allow everyone to contribute when brain storming solutions.
- Show respect when meeting to resolve even the smallest complaints
- Smile often, keeping humor ready and anger at bay.
- Remember that final solutions do not have to be reached in one afternoon. "Sleep on it", is a cliche for a reason, and provides the time needed to gain perspective.

Mastering the art of staying calm under pressure is a fine balance of removing yourself from the situation emotionally, while remaining engaged enough to complete the task.

One of the most profound moments in history where this occurred, was the moon landing of Apollo 11. Neil Armstrong was a premiere pilot to be sure, but no one knew how much so, until July 20, 1969.

The lunar module had only a specific amount of fuel to descend to the surface of the moon and reascend to meet the command module orbiting above. Any variance, requiring the use of more fuel, would mean the meticulously planned flight would be a disaster.

As the men approached the surface Neil noticed it was too rocky. He knew this could cause damage to the module or worse, invite a crash landing. So, he kept flying, with Houston looking on in horror as he past the projected landing site.

When the historic words were finally spoken "Houston, the Eagle has landed", there were some not-so-famous words uttered by Houston in reply. "You've got a bunch of guys down here about to turn blue." Neil had made a successful landing, and Houston was breathing again!

Even in the face of so many unexpected issues, he had remained calm. By removing the emotional element before it affected his abilities, he was able to complete the task without incident. He encountered an unplanned rocky surface and simultaneously handled the fuel gauge, the clock, and the view out his module window, all without screaming "Oh my god look at all those rocks! We're going to crash! We're going to die! Oh no!!"

If he had allowed the rush of emotional reactions to an intense situation invade his mind, he would have met with certain death. But fortunately, Neil is one of the most skilled pilots in the world, and success was at hand.

When the receptionist is juggling multiple tasks here on earth, the order of importance is as follows:

1. In-person client
2. In-person vendor/bike messenger
3. All callers expect personal and internal
4. Colleagues visiting the front desk
5. Colleagues calling the front desk

An example: A man arrives and signs in, setting his briefcase down and straightening his tie. Just as the phone begins to ring he starts speaking at the same time the caller is talking. Here, you would acknowledge the man standing in front of you with a smile and a nod while asking the caller to please hold. Attend to the visitor, then return to the caller. This is a very simple way to look at multitasking, but it works.

If you step back and remember the "order of importance" and disengage the emotional component of the stressful situation, you will be able to handle any crisis, just as Neil Armstrong did when landing on the moon.

On the following pages are some sample dialogue scripts to further illustrate how to answer the phone, take messages, greet guests, resolve conflict and stay calm.

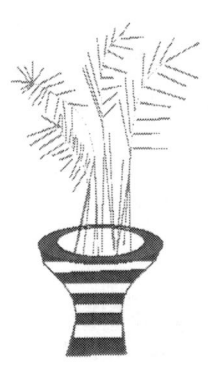

TELEPHONE DIALOGUE

RIGHT:

"I'm sorry I don't see a listing for that name. Would you care to speak with someone else in that department?"

WRONG:

"Oh yeah Sandy, she lost her job last week."

RIGHT:

"Could you give me your phone number anyway, just in case?" (as you rewrite your message)

WRONG:

"OK, she's got your number then, bye." (name is forgotten, no phone number was retrieved, no message is taken)

RIGHT:

"I apologize my switchboard is becoming very busy, may I place you on hold another moment while I try to find that number?"

WRONG:

"I don't have time to look that up. Suzy can, just a minute." (blind transfer)

RIGHT:

"I'm sorry to keep you holding so long, do you want me to search more directories or transfer you directly to Mr. Scott's voice mail?" (Give the caller a choice)

WRONG:

"Look, I'm doing the best I can, hang on."

LOBBY DIALOGUE

RIGHT

(Acknowledge the client as they enter the door)

"I'm Don Jones here for Mr. Scott"

"Great! If you wouldn't mind signing in I'll give Mr. Scott a call to let him know you've arrived"

WRONG

(Head down, looking up after the person has arrived at the front desk.) "Who are you here for?"

RIGHT

(Smile and nod as Mr. Scott leaves the office) "Good night Mr. Scott, have a nice evening"

WRONG

(Talking on personal cell phone) "God, I was so drunk last night" (Wave at Mr .Scott as he leaves while remaining on your personal call.)

RIGHT

(Smile and nod at the bike messenger) "How is your day going? I don't have an envelope up here yet." (look around the desk)

"Do you have the name of the person who called to request a pick up and I'll check with them to see if it's ready"

WRONG

(Stare right through the bike messenger with no smile) "A pick up? I don't know. If you don't see an envelope I guess there isn't one for pick up" (Back to personal call)

Breaks

Time away from the reception desk is coveted and should be honored by your relief receptionist. Unfortunately, this almost never happens. In nearly every position I have held as a receptionist this has been the number one angst for me.

The reason there is such resistance and poor attitudes toward giving a receptionist a break, is because the relief receptionists are usually busy, don't like answering phones, and most likely don't know how. This makes it unpleasant for them, so they try to avoid it any way they can. Sadly, the receptionist pays for this. But you simply must stand your ground. As with your reception job, every other job in the world contains tasks people would rather not do, so relief receptionists either need to deal with it, or find a job that doesn't require giving a receptionist a break.

We are human, and sometimes our co-workers forget that. Gently reminding others that we do not have the luxury of leaving our post, so as to attend to personal matters, restroom visits, and get a cup of coffee, will help them understand the importance of consistent, punctual break times.

If this does not work, you must notify your supervisor. The law requires that you receive breaks during your work day. This isn't a "bonus" but an entitlement. By kindly letting your supervisor know, the problem should be resolved by the time your next break rolls around.

CHAPTER 4
GETTING YOUR DESK ORGANIZED

Here is a list of items
receptionists in all offices
should keep at their desk:

- compact mirror (for finding the veggie burrito bits stuck in your teeth)
- tissues, napkins and paper towels
- bottled water, granola bar, and plastic utensils
- band aids, lint brush, nail file, safety pins
- foot powder, light fragrance and a make-up bag
- 6x9 white ruled pad of paper
- box of pens (to hide away when your current supply walks off)
- paper clips, binder clips

These items are essential if something arises and you cannot leave your desk. Being prepared for an unexpected late break, can help while waiting for your relief to arrive.

Staying comfortable will allow you to maintain your happy disposition and in turn allow you to remain at the top of your game.

A reception desk is similar to an information desk because it is the central component and hub of the office. Therefore, it is always a good idea to be prepared for any question or inquiry.

Most offices now have internet access. Even still, it's a time saver to look up what you may need to know in advance and type out a list for easy reference.

Here is a list of possible inquires a receptionist may field:

- Addresses and phone numbers to local restaurants, hotels and florists.
- Directions to local area land marks for out of town visitors.
- Emergency numbers such as poison control and building security
- Phone numbers, costs and hours of operation of nearby parking garages
- Taxi cab service providers.

Organizational tools such as a small desk calendar can be useful to keep reminders in one location. You may want to record upcoming meetings, travel dates, and catering orders for a luncheon.

This may seem like an elementary idea, but the nature of reception work does not allow for time spent unraveling a complex organizational system. Simple is better. Simple is easier. Less steps equal less mistakes.

Darienne Page (ROTUS), has a great system when meetings take place near or in the oval office. As you can imagine security is a top priority and so as guests arrive they are asked to leave their pagers, cell phones, and blackberries with her before proceeding to their meeting. She uses a post-it note and hand writes their name on it, attaching the note to the respective electronic device. Then she places all the devices in a large wicker basket on her desk. World

leaders come and go and this
simple procedure is consistently
reliable and more than sufficient.

Another reason organization is
important at the front desk is for
aesthetics. If you've ever walked
into a reception area where there
are too many nick-knacks and post-
it notes stuck on computer
monitors, telephones and counters,
you will instantly recognize this
is not a professional look.

To avoid this, decide what
information you most frequently
refer to throughout the day, and
type it up and print it out, with
clean clear fonts and bullet
points. Carefully tape this
underneath the counter of your
desk. If you do not have a
counter, consider obtaining a
clear desk mat to cover your
information sheets. You will
still be able to see it, yet it
will keep your desk looking neat.

Another idea is to print out your
information sheets and have them

laminated. They can be handled multiple times a day and remain crisp and clean. You can even spill coffee on them and they easily wipe clean. Some feel this is expensive, however the expense of several pads of post it notes, pens, tape and paper used to reprint your lists and notes is more so.

Keeping the lobby neat and tidy begins at the reception desk. Make sure you wipe down phones and computer keyboards with appropriate cleaners and sanitizers. Even with a one-man front desk, the receptionist shares her desk with various relief receptionists. These colleagues may have a cold or the flu, or may even decide to eat a cheese sandwich while relieving you for lunch. Which makes these wipes, disinfectants and cleaners indispensable.

CHAPTER 5
TELEPHONES AND TECHNOLOGY

Acquiring basic typing skills is
essential if you want to use
today's telephone equipment at the
pace in which most front desks
operate. "Hunt and peck" will get
you no where fast. Most support
positions in the workplace require
a minimum of forty words per
minute. Time yourself right now.
Maybe a refresher course at your
local community college is all you
will need to improve your typing
speed.

Here are the two main phone
systems you will see at a
reception desk:

- soft console (digital)
- PBX (analog)

Both types of phones have the same primary function: To receive multiple incoming calls and to transfer those calls to multiple extensions.

Both have a physical phone, and a console. The digital phone has a "soft" console which means it is a computer. The analog phone has a "hard" console which means it is a physical device, not a computer and is attached to the physical phone.

The digital phone system has the office directory held in a database on it's "soft" console. By typing the name of the person for whom the caller is looking, you can then select it and transfer the call.

This is a great idea in theory, but in practice, unless you have the exact spelling of the person's name, it will not pull up the listing. Several tries may be necessary until you memorize everyone's name.

But once you do locate the correct name, the system is quick and impressive. You simply push the "enter" key on the computer keyboard and the caller disappears instantly. With this system you no longer have to manually dial extensions.

The downside to this very slick method of call transfer, is that you can't get the call back if you made a mistake and selected "Brad Cummings" rather than "Branden Cummings". Unfortunately with the ease of call transfer, comes the ease of errors.

Knowledge of your office mates, and good solid typing skills are crucial with this type of phone system.

The analog phone system is typically found in a smaller office. Unlike the digital phone, this entire system is separate from any computer at your desk. The console has rows of lights corresponding to all the extensions in the office. If the light to a corresponding extension is lit up, this indicates the person is on the phone or has their phone on "do not disturb" or DND. This is a very handy feature, so as to know if a person is on the phone already prior to transferring an impatient caller.

The method of transfer with an analog style phone is all manual. After answering the call you simply push the "transfer" button, the extension number, and the "release" button. All analog phones are different, but this description fits most.

With the analog style, even after the transfer, the caller stays on your line until it is physically connected to the line to which you transferred them. This is great because it allows you to correct incorrect dialing before the caller disappears. (unlike the soft console)

Headsets are not for everyone. If they aren't high quality and comfortably fit to your ear, you won't be able to hear the caller. Straining like this for an entire eight hour day can drive you crazy. Keeping these sanitary is also a chore as is wiping down the handset multiple times a day.

My recommendation is to use the handset, unless you are on a high call volume switchboard. Using a hand set also allows visitors to see when you are on the phone and know whether you are speaking to them or to a caller. This will avoiding uncomfortable situations. *Are you talking to ME?!*

CHAPTER 6
THE FUTURE LOOKS BRIGHT

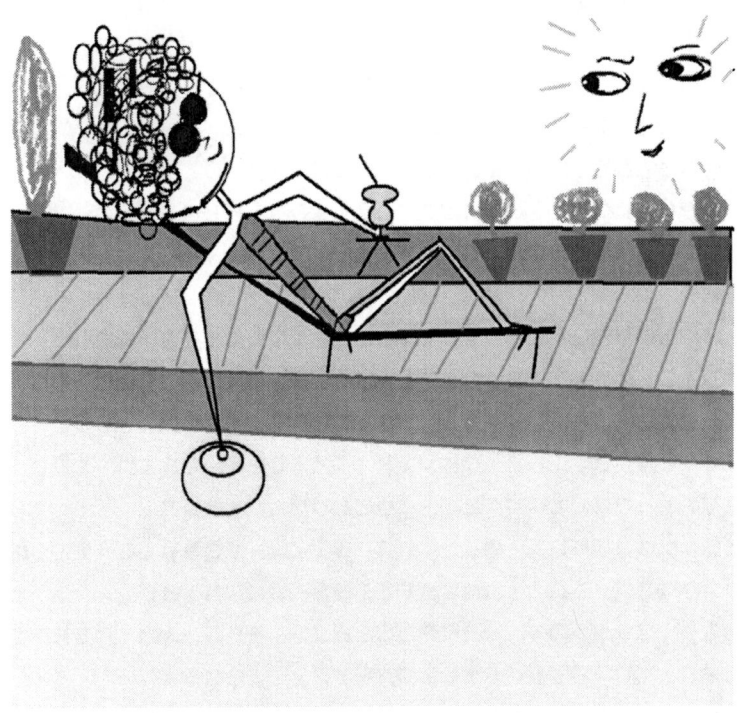

Bureau of Labor Statistics

Below are the projections for the receptionist in the coming years as published by the Bureau of Labor Statistics. According to the most recent report, the future looks bright, and the possibilities endless.

Employment is projected to grow faster than the average for all occupations. Job growth, coupled with the need to replace workers who transfer to other occupations or leave the labor force, will generate a large number of job openings for receptionists and information clerks.

Employment of receptionists and information clerks is expected to increase by 15 percent from 2008 to 2018, which is faster than the average for all occupations. Employment growth will result from growth in industries such as offices of physicians and in other health practitioners, legal services, personal care services, construction, and management and technical consulting.

Technology will have conflicting effects on employment growth for receptionists and information clerks. The increasing use of voice mail and other telephone automation reduces the need for receptionists by allowing one receptionist to perform work that formerly required several.

At the same time, however, the increasing use of other technology has caused a consolidation of clerical responsibilities and growing demand for workers with diverse clerical and technical skills, such as virtual receptionists. Because receptionists and information clerks may perform a wide variety of clerical tasks, they should continue to be in demand. Further, they perform many tasks that are interpersonal in nature and are not easily automated, ensuring continued demand for their services in a variety of establishments.

Median hourly wages of receptionists and information clerks in May 2008 were $11.80. The middle 50 percent earned between $9.69 and $14.44. The lowest 10 percent earned less than $8.09, and the highest 10 percent earned more than $17.07.

My fellow receptionists,

Reception work can be difficult at times, and is hugely underrated. However, with hope, vision, and perseverance, we can change the way the receptionist is viewed in the workplace. If you take even one piece of advice I've laid out here in this handbook, I believe together we can show the world what true professionals receptionists can be, and what an integral part we will play in the future of corporate America.

Sincerely,

Lisa Harmon

ABOUT THE AUTHOR

Lisa Harmon is a receptionist and writer who lives in the Seattle area with her dog Princess. She is currently at work on her first novel.

FURTHER READING

The Receptionist
By Joyce Twing

Surviving the Workplace: A Guide to Emotional Well-being
By Gary Cooper and Ashley Weingberg

The Little Book of Stress Relief
By Dr. David Posen

How to Dress for Success
By Edith Head and Joe Hyams

A Touch of Grace: How to Be a Princess, the Grace Kelly Way
By Cindy De La Hoz

The Professional Secretary's Handbook
By Mary Devries

Typing for Beginners
By Betty Owen

My Little Golden Book of Manners
By Peggy Parish

CPSIA information can be obtained at www.ICGtesting.com
Printed in the USA
LVOW05s2144070114

368468LV00032B/981/P